Love fro

Pleiades

Written and channeled by Kate Sparks

Illustrations by Jeff Jacklin

Table of Contents

Dedication

This book is dedicated to all of the Starseeds on Earth. May we move into the new paradigm with ease and grace.

In the starlight, love always,

Kate

In Gratitude

My husband, David: His love and faith have helped bring this book into the physical.

Jeannine Murphy: Her friendship and confidence helped this book flow. Her encouragement along the way supported my vision.

Jeff Jacklin: He is a kind and gentle man who draws beautifully and was extremely patient with me. He brought my etheric visions of my Star Family to paper.

Topaz Abbott: She is a great teacher and my friend. Her guidance and support have encouraged me to write this book.

Ziranna Dix: The energies that she holds in love, peace and joy helped me open as a channel.

David Miller: His dedication to personal and planetary healing has been an inspiration to me.

My good friends: Mary Ann and Clint Dohrman; Kim Best and Dr. Tuck Hayes; Holly Coffey and Beryl May.

My Seven Sisters: Their love and friendship are unconditional and constant. Special blessings to Kathryn Baruah, Lesley Chailler, Bernadette Kristaponis, Karen Poulson, Lin Prucher, KayAnne Riley and Pauline Taylor.

My Brothers: Their support and encouragement are ever present. Love to Ari Budnick, Francis Leitao, Jeff Neal, Roland Reed, Mike Ringhouse and Matthew Turner.

♡

♡

Part One: Kate

Homesick

I wondered why I struggled here so much. And it took me awhile to figure out that duality is not my true home. It was not so much that I disliked it here as that I was missing where I came from. I have always been homesick. I feel lonesome, especially in a crowded room. I feel loving companionship when I am by myself.

I always wanted to be left alone. I did not want to be lonely. I was never left alone and I was lonely.

There was a massive sense of loss within me. But what did I lose? Where could I find it?

I came to Earth not remembering how to participate in duality. I was naïve, thinking if I just loved my family more, they would be nicer. That made sense to me. I did remember love's power. That did not work though, that power frightened people. Love actually frightened people. Ah, yes, now I remembered duality.

I became fearful being love.

Love has played many roles in my life. Some of them were not so pleasant. It took a large portion of my lifetime to see love clearly as love and nothing else.

Some beings come here with great joy, they are happy here and that has always surprised me. I wondered, "How are they happy, how do they fit in? How do they do it? Well, how do they?" And most importantly, "What is wrong with me?"

There was more to me, but where was it? How could I find it? How could I get out of here?

This Self has never really wanted to be here, my Higher Self wants me here. My Higher Self is ecstatic with all the learning; this Self has not found it so fun.

My mission is nearly completed; time is speeding up, it won't be long, I am almost Home.

As time is speeding up, my vibration is also. I know that Home is a vibration. To me it is also a place, the Pleiades. When I vibrate at the fifth dimensional rate, here in the third dimension, I will be Home. I will be Home and on the Pleiades.

Living on Earth

I was told many times to not be so sensitive and to harden my heart. I worked at lowering my sensitivities and found that got me into a place of deeper angst. I came here with an open heart. But the wounds came faster and quicker than I had thought they would and my little body and undeveloped Earth mind at one and two years of age did the best it could, it closed up for protection. I had to survive and knew that if I opened up, I would surely die of a broken heart.

It is interesting that people thought my heart was open, but really it was not. But really it was. It was and it was not. For me, a Pleiadian in the heart energy, it was closed; from the Earth people's perspective, it was viewed as open.

I knew my birth home was temporary, so I held the idea of escaping. Maybe it was summer camp or a weekend with my grandparents. Short term escapes for now, and then I'd make them longer until I was finally free and away from the brutality.

I struggled through the years and did everything I could to go undetected. I adjusted, kept quiet, accepted this life and played the game to keep myself alive and get out. I survived my sentence with my family and finally got to be alone.

I was mostly free from my family, and alone, but I was still homesick.

My life continued to be difficult as my wounds caught up with me and took their toll. I knew that I had to heal. The homesickness was puzzling because all my life I had wanted to leave my Earth family and home and yet I was homesick.

How could that be? But there it was as always, strong and undeniable.

Duality has been a good teacher and I have learned many things. But most of the things I don't care to share. The exciting part, the glorious part that I feel like sharing is a portion of my mission and purpose here.

I now jump to the breaking point of nowhere to run and so much to do.

Where am I from? Who am I?

The Pleiadians Arrive

It didn't take but a few seconds. My internet search came up with different stars where one could be from along with the name of a fifth dimensional channel. I made the appointment and knew all was right. I listed my five or so questions for the channel and called at the meeting time. The main questions were: where am I from, do you know I am homesick, and how do I get back?

I made the call and at that second when I heard my Ascended Teacher speak, my Earth life shifted and thankfully would never again be the same. I would not and will not go backwards. Feelings of joy from my fifth dimensional Self, Oshala, flooded into me as well as from my Teacher, Personal Guide and Soul Family Member. I could feel the confirmation that there was more to me than what was here. It was a huge, powerful moment and the words are etched in my mind.

"Greetings, I am P'taah. I am one of the Masters and one of the Teachers in the Pleiades. We are a great place, we are a beautiful place. We do not have the violence, we do not have the pollution, we do not have the duality that the Earth does. It is a place of unity and love and it is *that*, that is what your heart longs to reconnect with."

P'taah touched my heart. His love is so pure and unconditional that I felt it was safe to open some of my heart to him. He found the small opening and brought his magnificent light to me. It was a light that I know so well, that I was familiar with, that I longed for. There he was, finally. My family was here. My heart told me first. I felt it, then heard and then remembered.

To this day, I repeat P'taah's opening words daily, sometimes several times, with great enthusiasm and strength. Every time I feel my heart open and more love pour in. There is the sadness though, as always. Why was he not here, why am I alone, why doesn't he visit me? And then the anger: why was he not here, why am I alone, why doesn't he visit me? The questions were always the same, the emotions changed around them. P'taah is here, I am not alone but yet it is not the same.

You might be thinking that since I made the Pleiadian Star Family connection all would be right. It was not. The years of abuse and neglect, some from others, some from me, all of which I created, gave way to years of work.

My life experiences had been a driving force to find Home. I don't know if the homesickness will ever go away, but it has lessened as I know more of who I am and where I came from. I know my real family and I know where I am going back to.

The Illusion

I happily and sadly knew the one phone call would lead to many trials, healings and emotional outbursts in every direction. But P'taah loves unconditionally and is committed to me and my life. He told me he would stay with me and so he has.

Together we go through this life, hand in hand; he in love for all, with me always asking, "P'taah, may I come Home now?"

P'taah tells me, "You are Home. I am with you on the Pleiades right now."

I ask him, "When? When will I completely be Home?"

He replies, "Soon."

I press further and ask, "When is soon?"

He replies, "Very."

P'taah patiently waits until this Self vibrates high enough and wakes up to really know, "I am Home, I am in the Pleiades and I am on Earth. I know it, I feel it and I see it." And then with love, this Self will leave its participation in duality.

In the meantime, I struggle with the illusion of separation and not fully being Home. I desire to return to the non-dual Oneness, but in order to do so I must actively participate in duality to accomplish my mission and ascend. There is no "time" in the Oneness, but time is both running out and dragging on endlessly here in duality. My greatest solace through it all is my connection to the fifth dimension, my Star Family and P'taah.

It won't be long now. I can feel myself rising above the illusion and detaching more and more. I feel it. And I know it, and soon I will see it.

Please Write a Book

Whispers in my ear: "Write a book. Please, write a book."

I kept thinking, "Write a book? What would I write a book about? I don't want to write a book."

Then the whisper said louder, "Write a book. It is your mission."

As an active participant in this illusion of duality, this mission rang true to me. So I sat down to write a book and thought, "Well, I have nothing to write about. My life is ordinary and average. I am certainly not going to write about the lower things I have experienced and I never thought I had many noteworthy experiences."

I asked, "So what on Earth am I going to write about?"

Then I heard Spirit say, "Well, you are not going to write about Earth, you are going to write about your Star Family."

"Oh, okay," I thought, "Well, I could do that. I could write about my brothers, Aaron and BoStro, and P'taah. I could do that."

It was harder than I thought. It was difficult in that I had never channeled for myself, let alone myself for myself! And, what do I write about my Earth life? No one wants to read about that, I don't particularly like thinking about it myself.

Sananda says, "Don't look back, unless you want to go there."

And I don't want to go there. So, how could I talk about why I wanted to connect with my Star Family unless I wrote a bit about my Earth life? That did not sound fun for me. And once again my Higher Self was ecstatic.

I continued to talk myself out of writing the book by thinking, "Do I really know much of the Pleiadians and their life? Do I really know anything that people would be interested in reading?"

Then I heard Spirit say, "Introduce the Pleiadians individually and bring them more onto the Earth."

"Ok, I can do that."

Then Spirit said, "Can you do that with love?"

I thought, "Well, what does that mean? I am loving. Of course, I can do that."

And Spirit said, "Can you write the book and love yourself?"

I did not know what Spirit meant until I sat down again to write and channel and discovered I had no remarkable teachings to bring forth, no great revelations. That did not feel very good to me. And that was my ego. I had told myself that I must bring forth new fifth dimensional knowledge so I could be of service with life changing information.

Then I heard, "Right now, that is not your mission."

Again I heard Spirit say, "Will you bring the Pleiadians more onto the Earth and have unconditional love for yourself?"

"Yes, I can do that. I will write the book. I will write the book as an introduction to my Star Family. Plain and simple, I will honor myself for what comes forward and accept with love and perfection."

Visiting with the Pleiadians

I have been, in full waking consciousness, astrally visiting the Pleiades and the fifth dimensional ships for many years. Through my third eye, I have seen both my brothers, BoStro and Aaron. I have also seen Mira and Harmon. To my dismay, I have not seen P'taah, but everything doesn't happen for a reason.

I kept hoping during the writing of this book that I would see the other Pleiadians that were channeled but are not pictured here. Well, I have not seen them. I know their energy and they say that is what is most important for now. I have a clear picture of the four Pleiadians I saw. My artistic talent does not currently include drawing faces. In order to put them on paper, I needed an artist to sketch them from my description. Spirit led me to Jeff Jacklin. He has done excellent artwork. He drew with such kindness and detail, helping me to bring their appearance onto the Earth.

I channeled all the Pleiadians, one by one. They were voice channeled along with automatic writing. In the channeling, they individually came through a corridor of fifth dimensional light and cohabitated with me.

When I astrally visit the Pleiades to spend time with my family, P'taah tells me that I must ask his permission and go with his supervision.

Just for fun though, to see if I can pull one over on P'taah, and because I know the answer already, I sometimes secretly whisper to BoStro and Aaron, "Shh. Don't tell P'taah I am asking. Let's surprise him... May I come and visit you both and then we will all go see P'taah?"

In the middle of our conversation, just as I start to ask the question, P'taah pops in and I hear "No, you may not visit them without my supervision."

I have long given up trying to figure out how P'taah always knows I am whispering to my brothers about a secret visit or other surprises that I thought would go unknown to him. I say this with love and humor, because if P'taah was not there listening, I would be devastated. But still I try to pull one over on him. I have never succeeded.

I have grown so accustomed to being with my beloved P'taah that I am surprised when someone asks, "Who is here? Who is the Ascended Master here?"

P'taah is always with me, I would only know if he were not there. I don't always sense that it is P'taah who is there, because he is always with me. Again, I would only know if he were not there. And that is something I do not care to experience.

The Star Family

I know I have lived in numerous fifth dimensional star systems, as many of you have. In this incarnation on Earth, I came from the Pleiades. It is part of my mission to speak of the Pleiadians and bring more of their energy and light onto the planet. These channelings are directed to everyone, not just the Pleiadian Starseeds.

Maybe if you do not resonate with the Pleiades currently, you will after reading this. And if you have never been there, you might give it a go in the after-Earth time. Some of the Pleiadians presented here may be new to you and some you may already know. You may wish to stay connected with some of them after this meeting. However it works, it is always perfect.

With passion and love, I introduce my Pleiadian Soul Family, including: my fifth dimensional Self, Oshala; my teacher and personal guide, P'taah; my brothers, Aaron and BoStro; and my other Soul Family members, Leia, Mira, Semjase, Randeau and Harmon.

Love always,

Kate

Part Two: The Pleiadians

♡

Mira

♡

Mira – Beauty and Love

Hi, this is Mira.

I am pleased to connect with you. I love you so much. You and I know each other, we are family and I am especially happy to make this connection today.

Your kind thoughts filled with light are being felt in the hearts of humanity. These kind thoughts in your heart are opening you to new ways of being and thinking. You are working with compassion in everything you encounter. This is a beautiful path and one that will lead you to more beauty and more love.

My love for you is in levels of joy. I experience the feeling of happiness when I think of you. Then, when I connect with your heart I am in a blissful state.

I am with you. I understand you. I love you.

I am Mira

BoStro

♡

BoStro – From My Heart to Yours

Hello, this is BoStro.

I am from the Pleiades. The Pleiadians are fifth dimensional beings from the Adam species. We are your ancestors and many of you reading this are star seeded from the Pleiades. We look human. We have the same higher vibrational energetic characteristics and traits that humans have. If I were to walk down one of the streets in an Earth city and you saw me, from my physical appearance you would think I was born and raised nearby or maybe I was a tourist from another city on Earth. If though, you felt my energy, you would probably guess I was not from Earth. My vibration is high and I have a clear, light way about me. I would feel different to you than most third dimensional humans.

My emotional body is all loving and I come from a place of heart unity. You would not sense judgment from me or a lower thought about any part of you. My mental thoughts are based in love and I hold compassion and honor for the humans on Earth. I am kind and respectful to all of who you are. I am spiritually advanced, like you are, and know that all we really are is love.

Do not, though, mistake my gentleness for poor boundaries. I am balanced in my masculine and feminine sides and would not have a problem saying "No" with love or removing any and all parts of myself from a situation based in fear and negativity. It is not my intention or desire to be in a lower thought field.

I am Kate's fifth dimensional, Pleiadian brother. We grew up together. We had, and even now are having, grand times in the Pleiadian high light. My sister and I were created in the same soul stream, next to each other. We are from the same Soul Family.

I have incarnated on the Earth and ascended. I have come from the higher dimensions, as my sister has, and I have stepped into the Pleiades. It is my home now.

Kate and I have a very close relationship in the Pleiades. We communicate telepathically. Whenever she sends a telepathic signal to be with me, at the same time, I am sending a signal to her. I always want to be with her, too! There has never been a time when I did not want to see my sister, when I did not want to be with her. We have always and will always love each other. We have never known, done, or will do anything other than love. When she connects with my energy, it is soothing and consoling. She remembers the feeling of Home through our connection and her loneliness from being in the third dimension fades away during our time together.

Her loneliness stems from feeling removed and isolated from us in the fifth dimension. It has thrown her into trauma and is hard on her heart. I tell her that my love is here and yet, she needs constant reassurance that we are here and we will not leave without her fully with us. I adore my sister, there is no other way my heart would lead me to feel about her. There is and always will be complete adoration.

We have had lives together on other planets and in other star systems. When we got ready to leave those places, we always wanted to go somewhere else together. In this lifetime we are working in, we wanted to go to a fifth dimensional star system, we wanted to go to a place of the Adam species, we wanted to go to a place that we could incarnate from and get back to easily. The Pleiades has a beautiful heart energy and we enjoy being here doing our soul work. We have other Soul Family members in the Pleiades with us.

I do everything in total joy and in love. I am always aware of my actions and what they will do. I am aware of my thoughts and what they will do. I am very aware that I am a creator. I am creating my thoughts and, in turn, creating my actions and I understand repercussions. All of you went to Earth to enhance your creative skills and were curious about creating in duality. I create in love; I do not create in fear.

My heart opens to you all and I send you love and blessings. I am always available for you to connect with, you may reach out and speak to my heart and I will reply with my love.

Some of you have been hesitant to open your heart. In many times and places, you have opened your heart only to have it hurt. The more you expand, the more you open to love, the less you can be hurt. If your heart is open fully there is so much love and compassion that when seeing lower behavior it will not be so hard on your heart. The lower energies can be filtered through an expanded heart and released.

I know that seeing things in duality is painful and that some beings on the Earth aim to hurt the heart. However, if you open your heart more, you will in turn become more loving and compassionate.

When you are not in love, you are in fear. One way this fear shows itself is in lower thoughts about yourself. On Earth, you are not taught to love yourself. You are taught to love others and be tough on yourself. Learning to love yourself has at times been difficult and quite a process.

You all have studied, learned and prepared for these lifetimes on this planet with high hopes of achieving your mission and fulfilling your purpose. Your Soul Family chose you and you volunteered; it was the same. The growth and expansion of your soul here on Earth will add to the soul weight of your entire Soul Family.

I don't feel sadness the way you might, but you could say that I experience sadness. It does tap on my heart to see suffering, to see sorrow. I see the divinity in all and know that you chose to be here, so your experiences are in your highest good. I know how important your mission is.

Many of you strive to be connected with us, for then you feel complete. Those of you who would like to connect with your Soul Family in the Pleiades, please call out to them. Send a ribbon of light to their hearts. They are here for you, hoping to make a stronger connection and be more involved in your life. When you connect, you will feel the love that you know and have missed.

Many Pleiadian Starseeds have taken a difficult path, a difficult mission. You are exploring themes of disempowerment, lack of trust and faith, and denial of your feelings. Many of you have learned what happens when feelings are denied and have in turn experienced the consequences. Many of you have also learned what happens when you don't speak up.

The awakening to the fifth dimensional light is also part of your mission. Please recognize this accomplishment, for in this dense energy it is quite a task. I have been calling my family on Earth for many of their lifetimes only to have my words go unheard or unanswered. Your soul glows in this connection to Star Family and you have grown with this small but significant part of your mission. This connection has also helped you increase your personal power for you know more of who you are.

At times, living in duality has been a painstaking process, but all your souls have grown and evolved. You are galactic anthropologists and share with us what you are learning in duality. When I check in with you in your dream times, you are all quite pleased with your learning here. I do see in your waking consciousness that you are not so pleased and often do not call these experiences "learning". I value your work and am grateful that you are here. I thank you.

Many of you incarnated with the intention of being a teacher: a teacher on Earth and a teacher in the higher dimensions. This realization has been a long path, for when you were young, the idea of teaching was not in your image of who you were. Your definition of a teacher has evolved and many of you have realized that you are teachers in a non-traditional sense. Not completely knowing your purpose has made your life an interesting challenge, but you have not given up. You have all become stronger and gaining strength was part of the mission.

You all share different variations on the same lessons. One lesson is to stay in the now. I know that many of you like to look back. You are also continually learning acceptance and I hear you say to yourself, "Well, I accepted that." And then you experience the lesson in a different way and practice acceptance again. You are always working at loving yourself because, as you know, there are many on the Earth who would prefer that you not love yourself. These may seem like simple lessons, but I tell you, you have been working on them in many lifetimes.

Quite often, the Starseeds are critical of themselves because at times they are comparing their third dimensional

Selves to their fifth dimensional Selves. They are hard on themselves for not being awake earlier in their lives even though that was the divine plan. You agreed to experience what it was like to incarnate on this planet asleep. We look at you as highly evolved beings having an experience in duality. We see the great light that you hold and carry. You will hear from other Pleiadians in this book who will say the same thing. I will tell you first, please do not be hard on yourself. It is hard on your heart and unloving towards Self.

It is difficult to verbally convey the love I have for you all. Words are not adequate. So I again invite you into my heart and you will see how I hold you in the divine light of perfection.

There are many Pleiadians who are interested in the feelings that can be experienced on Earth and they are interested in the high-level sensitivities of the Starseeds. It is challenging for those Pleiadians who have not incarnated onto lower vibrational planets to understand. The Starseeds send these feelings and thoughts back to us for processing and to then spread this knowledge throughout the galaxy, which assists other third dimensional places in their evolution. The Starseeds are giving other fifth dimensional students the opportunity to learn about duality without having to incarnate on Earth or other third dimensional places.

In duality, you all have learned that your sensitivities and high-level feelings are both good and bad and you have learned the conflict of having these gifts. You have learned what it is like to turn these gifts off and what it is feels like to turn them on. Turning them off was good and bad, and turning them on was good and bad. You all know duality.

And as I said earlier, you have learned consequences, in particular the consequences of leaving the planet early. Many of you have ascended before, but it was not a whole ascension; parts of yourselves were left behind in your hurry to leave. This has happened to some of the Starseeds, so you agreed to return to Earth in the physical for the Ascension and to gather these scattered parts and make a whole ascension.

Many of you were in Atlantis and saw the pain and suffering there. Some beings there helped you misuse your spiritual gifts that you brought with you then. Others deceived you with their intentions. That caused you to close down your gifts, personal power, knowledge and feelings. Some of those who betrayed you claimed to be spiritual. This also saddened your heart.

As your guides and teachers have explained in this lifetime and others, you are here to gather these gifts and parts of yourself, knowing that it would be a difficult path. Some of you may feel the lack of certain gifts in your life now, but there is no lack; they are yours. Please call them closer to you and take ownership. We are a step removed and see who you are. If you knew who you really are, you would be amazed and so very pleased.

We see the rings of light around each of you from every lifetime: every piece of information, every thought and every action. They affect all your lives, all parts of yourself, all the people you have ever met and all the places you have been. It is a marvelous sight.

You may have wondered why your Soul Family or your Star Family doesn't bring a ship down to rescue you. We could, but we won't, because we love you. You and we are working for your final Ascension, for the evolution of your soul. Your

Star Family has never left you. We have always been close and we always will remain close.

My desire for you all is that you remember more of who you really are and love yourself and this life wholeheartedly.

Many of you want to return to us now, but you all know the importance of completing your mission and fulfilling your purpose. We smile at the paradox: when you have completed your work, you will be comfortable on Earth, but that is when you will be called back Home.

My love always,

I am BoStro

P'taah – Joy

Greetings, greetings, this is P'taah.

You know, Dear Ones, you might be surprised about why you came to Earth. And yes, I hear you telling me all kinds of reasons. I listen and then I tell you the real reason you came back. And you can barely believe it!

But I continually tell you, you came back for the adventure! And you came back for the thrill of it all! You came to have fun! And yes, I hear your thoughts now and I smile.

I smile at your eye rolls, your sighs and your thoughts of "Really?"

I smile because I see the fun; I see where your adventurous mind has taken you onto paths of joy. I am looking at you all with the whole picture. The whole picture is joy because that is who you really are.

Do you remember being in grade school and then high school? And what do you recall from that? You don't really remember the bad cafeteria lunches or smelly gym clothes. What you mostly remember is the fun.

Yes, I know at times you have been in a lower state here on this planet. There has been sorrow in your life, I validate and honor your experience. But again, I lovingly tell you, you are here for joy. So when you leave here, you will remember joy. Joy is permanent, pain is fleeting.

In joy,

I am P'taah

Leia – Life is Great

Hi, hi, hi. Hi, hi hi, hi, hi! This is Leia!

I'm here! Boy, what a treat for me today! I have been trying to get to talk with Kate, to be closer to her, for awhile now.

You know, she's kind of like my sister on the other side. She's older than me; she's my older sister... kind of like a mother—the relationships are different in the Pleiades. It's different than on the Earth. But we're very close there. I'm so happy to be with her today. And you too!

Yes, my life is great, my life is exciting. I live in the Pleiades. I'm about fourteen years old here. I'm in school. And school is great; school is fun. I like it so much. I'm very energetic and enthusiastic and I have joy all day long. I don't know anything else really. I, well, I do know, you know, the duality and the denseness, but I don't participate in that. I don't go into that.

I'm with a lot of my friends here. I'm with a lot of teachers and Masters also. I get to talk to anyone I want to. I get to be with anyone I want to. I am working on my creative skills here. I am learning about the Earth, but really, it's not that enjoyable. A lot of lessons about Earth are scary and sad.

I rise above it, but I can also feel the feelings of my friends on the Earth; I have lots of Pleiadian friends on the Earth. I see sometimes how sad they are and how stressed out they are, and I am happy to be here. I am happy they are on Earth because that's where they wanted to be, that's where they're learning, but I'm not going there for a very long time. I don't even think I would go to the Earth. I might pick another planet that is on the verge of Ascension, but I don't know. The Earth is on the verge of Ascension and look what is going on there. No, I don't think I will go.

I come down to visit Kate now and then, to be close to her third dimensional Self. But I'm happy to be here. I don't really think I'm going to incarnate outside the Pleiades and the fifth dimension. I like where I am now. I can go and visit Sananda and Mary any time I want to. And you know, Kate can, too. She is getting really good at astral travel and at the other parts of her mission that will help her return Home to us. It won't be long before I can embrace my sister fully.

You don't have to be in the third dimension to learn about compassion and feelings. I'm working on that now. When I visit with her, I don't take on all the feelings that she has because it would overwhelm me.

P'taah knows about those feelings and can be closer to her. He can share and talk about them, but you know, that's why she came to Earth, to experience it in the physical. I can't. I don't want to do that. So I don't have that very, very deep level of compassion.

I'm not allowed to incarnate on a third dimensional planet now. I have to be in school more and I have to study more and I have to be older. I have to be a bit more mature. But, you know, I love who and where I am now. So, I've not been on the Earth and I'm really quite happy about that. I see what's going on and I see all the stress and struggles. And quite frankly, I don't want to go. I am very happy here.

I just love my life. You know, on the Earth, I see people very excited about being in first grade and then when they get to third grade, they're like, "How embarrassing, I was in first grade." I think first grade is great. I think it's great wherever we are and I'm always supported. I'm always guided. I'm always loved wherever I am, but I look at Earth and I see people making fun of this person for being there and that person for being wherever and I don't want any part of that. I am supported here and loved unconditionally. So I can be free and have fun.

I see BoStro a lot. He's very fun. He's older than me. He takes care of me sometimes—and I take care of him sometimes, too! I bring him flowers. He is fabulous! He's always smiling and he's quiet and I connect with him in his heart and he's very special to me. (I used to have a crush on him.) I see Aaron a lot, too. He is quite charming! He is very good to me, too, of course!

We play spiritual games here. I have lots of friends, boys and girls. We play spiritual games; we practice our creative skills. We make meadows and streams and mountains and we work with crystals. We have wands that help us do the magic that we learned in the Light Schools. I like to work with the fairies. I am very interested in the elementals. So we create different areas, different grasses, waters and fields so the elementals can come in and play and we can work with them and learn from them. That's a much easier way for me to be, a much easier way for me to learn—in fun! I don't want to learn through duality and denseness and polarizations. I like to learn here in the fifth dimension with the fairies.

I like flowers, bright yellow ones! We have colors here that aren't on Earth and I can't explain to you some of the colors, but I like a lot of the yellows and pinks.

I'm going to be coming to Earth more now to visit Kate and other Pleiadian Starseeds. This is just a very small, small part of who Kate is and who all of you are. I've visited her in other lifetimes and she knew me right away and we had fun then too. From her perspective now, it wasn't always so fun in this lifetime. But like P'taah said, she will remember the joy and that is what I will keep for her and me, too.

Well, I guess I'll sign off now. I'm going to create something fun today, as usual! I'm just not sure what. I'm having new ideas. I'm so happy to visit. I will return. You will know when I'm around; there will be great joy.

I am Leia. Bye!

Randeau – Heart Embrace

Hi, hello, this is Randeau.

I am a student of P'taah and a colleague of Kate in the Pleiades. I am pleased to be here today. I am excited to come through and work in this channeling session.

I am thrilled to be close to Kate, in her aura, and I am overwhelming her right now with my words and thoughts and excitement. I will slow down a bit so she can adapt and work with me and my energy. The vibrational rate is familiar to her, but my excitement is overwhelming her. As P'taah said, the Earth beings have had "thrilling adventures" and I am picking that up, too. It is thrilling!

I am calmer now and she is reading my mind. Now she is voice channeling as I am telling her that P'taah brought me here so I could work with her today.

This is a good practice for me, a good lesson. I am studying the Earth. I am studying the feelings and emotions of a third dimensional existence. I am studying all the things that she is experiencing on Earth. So, it's amazing to be here.

P'taah is close to me now. We came down a corridor of light from the Pleiades and we are now, at Kate's invitation, cohabitating with her. I have never cohabitated with a Pleiadian Starseed who is in the third dimension, let alone one who will channel me! She was so kind to invite me to come here, and P'taah agreed to escort me, so here I am. I'm in this corridor of light with our teacher, P'taah.

This is a wonderful experience. While I'm here in Kate's aura, I have a profound connection to her feelings and thoughts. It is live! I am interested in her vast amount and range of feelings. This brief cohabitation is something I have yearned for because I am gathering so much information and gaining knowledge about her feelings. The cohabitation is much more than what could be achieved with an astral visit to the Pleiades or conversation here or at Home. It is quite special to be so close to my colleague and friend.

At times words are a struggle for Kate because she prefers to interact telepathically. Vocabulary and speech, in describing her feelings, do not suffice. In the Pleiades, if we want a deeper connection than words would give us, we do a heart embrace. It is an exchange of love and emotions. It also lets us know all of who we are embracing. It is a much deeper exchange than words could ever achieve, and it is done with respect and admiration. We also use a Galactic language in the Pleiades along with telepathy.

With the heart embrace, nothing is hidden from either party. We do not view things with lower consciousness. I know some of you have had to hide your feelings on Earth and that has not been a comfortable experience.

There is great camaraderie among the Pleiadian students and Kate is remembering more of that now, as I am with her. We are lighthearted in our interactions and always wish each other goodwill in all our endeavors; that, too, she has missed.

Kate transmits information to us telepathically. I am also getting information from her aura right now. The corridor that we have set up is accelerating the flow of information. So it's easier to convey information now and she is more relaxed and can interact with me in a clearer state.

I see when she gets anxious and stressed. I am curious about this because I energetically see and know everything going on, I comprehend anxiousness and stress but do not feel them at my vibration. Now, I can feel them intensely in her aura and emotional body. I am also seeing where these feelings have affected her physically and hear what those parts affected are relaying to me. She gave me permission to interact with her third dimensional Self before I came today, so this is extra learning for me. It is going to help me advance in my work in the Pleiades and other higher dimensional places.

I'm studying emotions and feelings based in fear. We don't have the lower vibrations that permit and provoke these feelings. We don't have pain or suffering. Many of the students here are fascinated by emotions; we are somewhat envious that Kate is experiencing them. It is difficult for P'taah to tell us what the feeling of suffering is, what the feeling of heartache is, what the feeling of being verbally and emotionally abused is. We observe with empathy. My feelings and thoughts do not contain the lower energies of the third dimension and there is no one here in the Pleiades or in the other higher places who operates in that kind of energy.

We experience with great joy, but it's very different than what you know. It is not easy to describe our joy and our love because so much of the joy and love on Earth is conditional and short-lived. I see where Earth residents have the idea that joy is only for special occasions. That is curious to me. How could something so natural and marvelous be reserved with an appointment? We are always in joy, always in love. We also experience bliss, which I know Kate is greatly missing. When she is with P'taah she is in the bliss energy.

As I am cohabitating with Kate now, I can feel all her feelings, so many at once. They would overwhelm me if

P'taah weren't here supporting me with his energy. I can feel her sadness and anxiety. I can feel them going through her mind now and I can feel her memories of other feelings, too. I am still now receiving lots of information and she has given me permission to take all that I learn from this experience Home to process and share.

She still now is a bit sad because she can feel P'taah's energy close to her now and even though it's me speaking, she can feel him and she misses him so much. They have a very close relationship. And she's sensing his presence even though it's me here, too, because he has a very large presence in her life. And even though she can feel him and his love now, she is sad. It's interesting that feeling his love makes her sad.

P'taah is our teacher. He has been so good to me. He arranged this meeting between Kate and me. It's going to accelerate my learning and Kate's too. She can't process everything that she is experiencing in this lifetime, but when she makes her final Ascension, we will study this lifetime along with all her other lives on Earth. I'm going to take all this information back to her students and share with them in great detail what I felt, what I learned and what I experienced.

I have not been on the Earth. I am not sure I want to experience the vibrational rate directly, as Kate is. I am learning about it from a higher vibration, which is more to my liking.

P'taah has many levels of students and has special teachings for every one of us. We are all different so he molds the teaching to who we are. I have learned from my interactions with my Earth colleagues that this teaching method is rarely used on Earth.

I am about 18 years old. You might say I am shy, certainly not as vivacious as Leia. I am enthusiastic about learning and enjoy being in the Pleiades. In your terms, I would be referred to as being single. I am not old enough, nor am I interested in a physical relationship with a partner. I will be later on, but not now. I live with my Soul Family. For recreation, I engage in advanced games with my colleagues and friends using our telepathy and sensitivities. Although I am older than Leia, I still play! I am also interested in science and geology. I have been fortunate to have traveled to other star systems where I have studied their geology. Occasionally, with permission, I will bring back rocks and crystals to use in my research here. P'taah and several of the Pleiadian Ambassadors have also brought rocks and crystals to me from their explorations in the universe.

I am stepping back now, at P'taah's request. I am going back, up the corridor with him. I am so full of knowledge and information.

With love, thank you all and goodbye,

I am Randeau

Harmon

Harmon – Unity

Greetings of love, greetings of peace, this is Harmon. I am also known as Harmony.

My work in the Pleiades is facilitating and strengthening the connecting of the Lower Self to the Higher Self. That work is represented in my name, Harmony. My mission is to help humanity connect with their Higher Selves and maintain that connection in harmony. When I reach out to my students, when I see my students, I check in on their connection and quite often find it is not how I taught this lesson.

My students are often unaware of their Higher Selves. They ignore and sometimes deny their Higher Selves.

We had many meetings before their incarnations. They thought then they would always be connected to their Higher Selves, so they spoke to me of how things would be in perfect flow for them on Earth. But once they came down, they could not at times feel the connection to their Higher Selves, and they did not always work in ease and grace.

I have time and patience. I continually work to help my students in their connection with their Higher Selves. I see the sorrow that disconnection brings. I see the heartache when my students are not aligned with their Higher Selves. Sometimes students fight their Higher Selves. The Lower Self has taken charge. It has been this way for so long and in so many lifetimes that they may not even be aware that there is a Higher Self.

Some of my students believe the Higher Self is cold and distant because it is unaffected by the death of the third dimensional Self. But as I said, I have time and patience and I am working and will continue to work to help my dear students to make this connection and return Home.

I send down information in beams of light. I work in the light corridors to connect the Selves. I help the Higher Self come down to be with the Lower Self and sometimes, I help the Lower Self rise up to the Higher Self.

Kate knows she has been disconnected from her Higher Self. She has fought with the Higher Self, she has argued, she has gone against the Higher Self. She knows what it is like to go against it and she knows what it's like to go with it, and although she knows the Higher Self is going to learn, whatever the cost, she has realized that it is much easier to go in the flow of the Higher Self.

I have seen some of my students take on experiences that weren't really in the path of their lesson, even when Higher Self was directing them to an easier way, a cleaner, smoother path. The Lower Self broke away from the Higher Self and went onto a way that was not very pleasant.

The Higher Self can guide the Lower Self, with perfect timing, to the perfect place, a better place than the Lower Self could reach alone, because the Lower Self often acts out of fear. I work to bring love and ease to the Lower Self in the light of the Higher Self.

As all of you read this though, these lessons are in the past. We covered many of your lifetimes in these last few paragraphs. Now, you are all connected to your Higher Selves. The paragraphs above were a reminder of the perfect place you were in then and the learning you did to be in the next perfect place of now.

I am a Master. I am an Ascended Master. I have great joy and great love. I do not wish to incarnate into a third dimensional system again. I see the discordance. I see the struggle. And I see my students live through it all with the utmost appreciation, respect and dignity. My students know my love for them, but I will take this opportunity to tell you, "I love you."

You have done the work, you have the connection; treasure it. You are Ascended Masters; simply walk the rest of the way out of duality with your Higher Self by your side.

I wish you all harmony.

In love and peace,

I am Harmon

P'taah – Teacher of Light

Greetings, this is P'taah.

My name, P'taah, means "Teacher of Light." You, my students, are also Light Teachers. You are my beloved students and I take great pride in you. And I thank you for teaching Light.

There are great adventures that await you in the galaxy. Part of you is there already. You are having wonderful times here and there. And maybe sometimes you do not marvel at your life here, but I, P'taah, do. I see all the light work you have done, the love you have held and given, and the beauty in your heart.

I will be closer to all of you now. Your time in duality is almost complete and I would like to be with you, hand in hand, as we leave this agreement and move into a more perfected state of love.

I will be with you, in love,

I am P'taah

Oshala – Here and There

Greetings, this is Oshala.

I am Kate's fifth dimensional Self. I live in the Pleiades. I am also frequently on the Pleiadian space ships.

I am in contact with all the parts of myself. I have many lives on the Earth and am engaged in all of them. I am collecting information and knowledge from my selves. I am sending information and knowledge. I am sending healing and giving love throughout all.

While I am communicating with all the parts of myself in the third dimension, I am, of course, connected and in clear communication with our soul, Kate's and mine. I know when our soul is reaching out, going into deep meditation, or going into a private, quiet time. I follow the guidance of our soul and am in complete unity with all the higher parts of myself.

I am working on complete unity with my third dimensional Selves. The lower dimensions are at times a struggle for them and they are frustrated with the polarizations and with the illusion of the third dimension. I am not frustrated because I, Oshala, do not hold the lower vibrational energies of my Selves on the Earth. I am engaged but not attached.-

There are many teachers and guides helping me to retrieve and unify all the parts of myself and to lift myself up and out of duality. It is my goal to unify, and I know that I will succeed because I have the ability to see future time. Now, though, I still need to do the work and this channeling is part of my mission and part of Kate's mission in this lifetime.

I'm enjoying being here closer to my third dimensional self, Kate. I know Kate is enjoying it also. Channeling her fifth dimensional Self feels different than channeling other beings, because I am part of her.

Kate is also enjoying this time with her fifth dimensional Self as it is a reassurance of who she really is. The Earth is in a crescendo and linear time is, along with many other thought forms and beliefs, collapsing. Part of her lesson in this lifetime and others, though, is to see everything as perfect and divine and to vibrate at such a level that the denseness does not affect her.

It's quite fascinating to watch all the parts of myself on Earth. You might picture this as watching a very large movie screen and I am sitting in the audience with my teachers and guides. We are looking at the screen, flipping around to different parts of my many lives. We might hit the pause button and work with that part of myself. Then we un-pause and move on to the next life.

In the fifth dimension, I see the timeline of my third dimensional Self as linear. We look at the lives as a line that can jump around and then become a circle. This line is all connected. It's all equal, it's all balanced, and then it turns into a sphere and it turns into geometric shapes and alternate realities.

Your fifth dimensional Selves would also like to have a stronger connection with you. Call them more into your lives and you will be pleased with the relationship. Many of you are practicing multidimensional presence and are very near to knowing and seeing your lives here and there and everywhere.

I am connected with all of you reading this and I thank you for allowing me to be part of your life. We are related in more ways than you think. It will be fun to see how our time here expands in other directions and dimensions.

Love to "all" of you,

I am Oshala in the Pleiades and
I am Kate on the Earth

Semjase – Space Life

Greetings from Space, this is Semjase.-

I am a Commander in the Pleiadian Space Command. I enjoy being in space and am interested in space technology and travel. I have committed my assistance and love to the Earth and humanity.

A large amount of my time is spent in space on the different ships within the Command. I frequent the Pleiadian mother ship, the *Athena Alcyone* which is a huge ship, many miles long and wide. It's docked in the Jupiter corridor, a large area that can hold thousands of fifth dimensional ships. The Jupiter corridor is millions of miles long, which ensures our safe entry and exit. We can move in and out of there frequently and not be detected.

Today I am in a smaller ship, a beam ship. It is an oval disk, streamlined on the outside, and feels warm and pleasant inside. It is the size of a small house and six or seven people can work with ease here. All of my needs are met in the beam ship. There are several other Pleiadians here with me.

While I do spend a lot of time on the Command ships, either on my ship or other large ships in space, I do return to the Pleiades to fulfill duties and responsibilities that require a more physical presence.

I enjoy everything I do and am very pleased with my life in the Pleiades and on the ships. Quite often I stay on the ships for months at a time. The ships are very comfortable and some areas on the larger ships are replicated to look like home in the Pleiades. If you were to visit our ships in the physical, with full waking consciousness, most of you would not want to return to Earth. Although we do not have the need to eat or drink, we have areas on our bigger ships to store food and water in case we are called upon to transport people from Earth. We have different areas on the larger ships to assist with Earth human's needs. Everything we desire is here also.

The vibration inside and outside of our ship is fifth dimensional. It is a calm, high vibration centered in love. I hear some Earth people wonder, "Why would I want to be in a metal ship? That seems cold and unpleasant."

It is not. The vibration is congruent with our vibration, the Pleiadians. We are love and that energy is in, on and around the ship. So you may see technology such as our computers, but the vibration of these instruments is different from those used and worked with on Earth. Our technology is interacting with us and has sentient-like qualities. Therefore, the vibration of everything on the ship is high and loving.

We are studying and observing the Earth. We have been given permission by the Galactic Councils to, at times, energetically protect and interact with Earth and its inhabitants.

When our ships are near the Earth, they are in fifth dimensional capsules of light, which provide protection and cloaking. We always work in highly refined corridors of fifth dimensional light. Even though many of you would like us to appear, we do not visually make our presence known often. We communicate telepathically with the humans who know the truth of who we are and why we are here. Throughout various periods on Earth, we have been acknowledged and well received, enough so that we have landed many times and worked with our Earth Star Family. This is not the case in this now moment on Earth. Times always change; we will be widely accepted once again, soon.

Our ships are shielded from third dimensional energies. We keep the ship finely tuned in a harmonious frequency. Because the polarity on the planet is so intense, we have various shielding techniques such as thought forms and white light that nothing of a lower frequency can penetrate. We are aware at the slightest hint of negativity and even though we vibrate at a higher level, we must still use various forms of shielding. The negative energy has been given power by the humans and it has its own thought field around the Earth. We would never want to come in contact with that!

Most of us will not step onto the Earth because we don't want to get involved in the Earth's karmic cycle. We don't want to go into the Earth's incarnation cycles and be pulled into a third dimensional situation. We are happy working full time here in the fifth dimensional energy for Earth and our friends. Therefore, we don't come too close to the Earth.

I have special assignments from Sananda, who oversees the many higher dimensional groups working for the Earth. There are joint operations and our ships frequently interact. Earth and humanity are the main attraction in the galaxy. Even beings from other universes have parked in the Earth's atmosphere to watch the end of duality and to witness the Ascension of a planet.

We revere our Earth brothers and sisters. We keep a careful eye on those who do not have the highest intentions for you. Nothing will ever diminish our love and support for you. We are committed to your advancement and upliftment. You are our dearly loved family and we wish to be with you wholly.

With love, I am your space sister,

I am Semjase

Semjase – A Visit to My Beam Ship

Greetings, this is Semjase.

I would like to lead you to my beam ship for a brief visit. Since we work on a different space and time continuum, it does not matter when you are reading this. I can still take each of you to my ship individually.

Anyone reading this, you may come with me to my ship if you desire. This is a one-time opportunity. After you have visited once, the corridor to my ship will not open to you again.

If you would like to visit my ship, please prepare yourself before you read further. Of course, you do not have to accept my invitation. You can simply read this and stay where you are.

I, Semjase, am setting up a fifth dimensional corridor of light for you. I am overseeing the corridor. The corridor of light is a shimmering blue with specks of gold. If you have agreed, it will now encompass you, the bluish-gold is all around you, and now the corridor is becoming all white, a bright, sparkling white light. This corridor is connected to my ship.

On the count of three, you may lift your spirit body up and out of your physical body. I, Semjase, am in the corridor with you and I will escort you up to my ship.

One, two, three. You are rising up and taking my hand; we are moving quickly through the corridor.

It is a beautiful corridor of sparkling white light and you are with me, Semjase. This corridor goes around the entire ship.

As we reach the ship's door, it opens and I lead you into my fifth dimensional Pleiadian ship.

You step inside and I see how happy you are to be here. I see you are remembering being here. This experience is familiar to you. My crew is standing in honor of you and they are greeting you. You may embrace them if you would like.

My ship has large windows and now you are seated at what you would call the central command area—and no, you may not touch anything. Look out and see the beautiful Blue Jewel in the distance. You can see the beautiful waters. You can see the Earth's aura. At this point, some of you can hear the Earth. As you are looking out our windows and connecting with the Earth, I can feel your great love for it and your life there. You are sending good thoughts and wishes to all aspects of your life.

I know you are enjoying being here with us. I know you have missed this perspective and this energy. It is a whole new way of life up here, very comfortable and easy. It is a beautiful vibration.

We are moving the ship closer to Earth so you can get a closer look at this beautiful planet.

This ship is one of the ships you might glimpse at nighttime. We visit different areas at dawn and twilight when it is easier for us to go undetected. Right now, we won't go any closer to Earth than we are currently.

If you would like, you may get up from the control area and walk around the ship. You may look outside the other windows. You may greet some more of the crew. They are eager to speak with humans from Earth.

♡

Please take several minutes now to enjoy your visit. You are all beautiful beings and we are enjoying your energy and personality.

It's almost time for you to return to your Earth body. You may not realize that you have been teaching this ship and the crew what it is like to be on the Earth. Your visit here has been a gift to us. We have learned a lot from you in the short time you have been on the ship. We thank you.

We will now take your spirit body down the corridor of white light. This corridor is connected to and encompasses your Earth body. I, Semjase, am taking your hand. We are going down the sparkling, white corridor. Now we are over your Earth body. Your Spirit body is entering your Physical Earth body with full alignment and perfection. You are completely settled in your body.

I am giving you a blessing and I am closing this corridor as I return to my ship. You are now fully in your Earth body and I am back on my ship.

This was a one-time visit. After you have participated in this, the corridor will not open again to my ship.

I invite you to be with me closer, always. Look for me and my ship at nighttime. Look for the twinkling, white lights. Feel me sending my love to you. Fill your heart and look up.

We hear you, we are here.

My love,

I am Semjase

Oshala – Knowing Love

Greetings, this is Oshala.

I am helping my third dimensional Selves see through the illusion and fully reunite with me in the higher vibrations. Ideally, I desire this work to be done by my third dimensional Selves with enthusiasm and acceptance, knowing there is only the path of love. I openly share with you now, my Selves have not always been on that path. Quite often my Selves were scared and frightened of Earth happenings and had no idea how to process the complexity of duality.

I discovered when my Selves were not in love that they were in fear and fear has repercussions. My Selves have learned, like many of you have, to work with love's power and to not give it away to fear. My Selves came into the remembering and knowing that fear is controlling. Love is freeing.

Being and working in love on this planet has sometimes been a difficult task. I see and know how difficult it is at times to love those who have done harm.

Sometimes Kate wonders why we chose to incarnate. It is painful to see the tragedies on this planet. I would not know what they felt like unless I had a physical Self here. Without firsthand knowledge, I cannot help to facilitate healing for third dimensional beings and places. I cannot teach what I do not feel.

In love,

I am Oshala and
I am Kate

Aaron

Aaron – My View with Love

Hello! This is Aaron.

I have been waiting to be called upon to be a part of this book. I am Kate's Pleiadian brother, her soul brother. BoStro is also my soul brother. We have a tremendous love for each other and have a marvelous time together. We are always in tune and on the same vibration.

We are often together doing spiritual work and studies. We are interested in the third dimension and are working in various ways for the upliftment of the planet and humanity. BoStro does work with healing. Kate does work with the emotional body and what it's like to process feelings in duality. I work on the mental constructs and belief systems.

I hold a place on one of the Pleiadian councils, where I interact with the Earth beings on an etheric level and I get to be with Kate more while doing this work.

Kate didn't know it, but I was visiting her years ago. I was calling to her and I was reaching out to her. I was pleased when she saw me with her third eye during a conscious visit to the Pleiades. I saw her clearly and she saw me clearly. I know when she saw me, it was hard on her heart.

You might think, "Why would it be hard on her heart to see her brother?"

The perception of separation, the illusion of being apart from me was painful. She senses me and she talks with me, but she cannot reach out and touch me. She can't give me a hug. She can't play with my hair or embrace me, hold my hand, as she so often does in the Pleiades. I know how she misses that. I know it is difficult for her to be physically separate from us.

And I tell you now, please do not be hard on yourself. Being hard on yourself has consequences that are not helpful to you.

We tell her that there is no separation, but it's paradoxical to hear that when she knows that she is separate, separate in the physical. I am not there to give her an embrace. I am always embracing her heart, but for her, it's not enough. Since she saw me and knows my name, she can feel me even more.

I miss my sister, but not the way she misses me. I miss the part of her that is gone, but I can tap into that part anytime, and her fifth dimensional Self, Oshala, is here with me all the time.

I used to hear her emphatically state, "I miss you, but you don't miss me," and my heart would go out to her. I hear her heart longing to be fully back with us. I am devoted to my sister. There is no other way. I will do everything in my power to have her wholly and fully return to us.

I have empathy for my sister that she is living in duality, but I am very happy for her, too. She is learning. She will graduate and teach.

I often hear her thinking "Why would I want to teach about duality? Why would I want to teach about fear? I don't even need to be here."

She will have this information for future time, for future work, to teach, to help beings and planets rise up and out of duality.

There are some beings who like duality and the polarizations. It fuels them. The drama and trauma give them energy. However, there are other beings on Earth who want an end to duality. Leaving duality and the illusion is quite a task, but you all know the path, you are way-showers and this is one of the many reasons you came here.

In the Pleiades and other fifth dimensional places, everything is love. We don't argue; we don't fight; we don't disrespect each other; we don't have any lower thoughts or feelings about our brothers and sisters. We do not take others' energy.

Sounds nice, doesn't it!

Many of the Pleiadian Starseeds have grown tired of the duality but are staying in the truth of who they are and why they came here. All times are important on the Earth and they have always known that it is crucial to be the starlight, shining brightly always.

I am a Pleiadian Ambassador of Light. There is a Pleiadian Council of Light and I am an Ambassador in that council. I enjoy my position and the work it entails. We interact with Earth beings, some are aware, some are not. We are sending light energy in various forms to the planet and its inhabitants. We are connecting to the light workers and way-showers who hold key positions in government and society to anchor the fifth dimensional light that is coming at a rapid pace to the planet. These beings are finding new ways to hold, carry and implement this higher light.

I am also working closely with many Pleiadian Starseeds on Earth. They may not know my name, but they know the Pleiadian energy and they know my energy. I am working with their mental bodies and how they speak to themselves and others. Some of their thoughts and words are not of the highest vibration. We say this with concern and compassion because we see what these thoughts and words create.

When I see lower thoughts being transmuted, being shifted into love, I can see auras bringing in more light. Changing your thoughts to all love will transform you and the planet more into who you really are: love.

I invite you to see duality through my perspective. Call on me and I will offer a view through my eyes; with more love, more kindness, more gentleness, with loving strength. I would like to be involved in your lives, you are my Star Family and I love you always.

Sending you my love,

I am Aaron

♡

P'taah – My Life

Greetings, this is P'taah.

As you know, I am an Ascended Master. I live in the Pleiades. I have a wonderful life there and here, and all is filled with great joy and light.

I am a teacher in the Light Schools and enjoy my work very much. My focus is on relationships in the emotional work I teach. I am also skilled in space travel and am fond of math and science-related work.

I am always near my beloved Twin Soul and Twin Flame. I have a home in the Pleiades with my Soul Family. I also have children in my lineage. My children are extremely beautiful and make my life incredibly joyful. I treasure them and often find myself simply standing beside them in silence, holding their hands.

I work closely with the humans on the Earth. I am particularly connected with the Pleiadians on Earth, as this is part of my mission. I am a personal guide to many of you. You are my students here and there. I have incarnated on the Earth and ascended. I do know what life is like in a physical body on the Earth!

A large portion of my time is spent in space. I am working intensely with the Earth for the Ascension. For many reasons, I feel it is important for me to be physically close to the Earth. So, I often spend time in small beam ships or the *Athena Alcyone* which are nearer to the Earth than the Pleiades.

You may notice a difference in my energy as you are reading this. It is because I would rather be interacting with you

---

about your life and having a relationship in that manner. I would like to make it all about you. But this book is about life on the Pleiades so I share with you the basics of my life in the stars.

But this, too, is a way to be more with you. I would like a relationship with you and want to be close to you. So I will tell you this...you may call on me and I will share more of my life with you. We have more in common than you think.

Love from the Pleiades,

I am P'taah

Aaron – Life in the Pleiades

Hello! This is Aaron.

My life in the Pleiades is fantastic! I have tremendous fun and enjoy everything I participate in. I enjoy music and play the piano. I am particularly fond of Mozart. I'm a good dancer and can do many of the dances of Earth. Our dancing is a physical expression of our joy and light. Often the dancing takes us into the energy of bliss.

I have incarnated on the Earth and ascended. It is not my desire to return to a third dimensional planet.

I work in the Light Temples and the Pleiadian Schools of Light, sharing and teaching my wisdom through my space adventures and council duties. I work with crystals from the Pleiades and other star systems. I enjoy connecting with my family on the Earth who are also my students and apprentices in the Pleiades.

I live in a beautiful place, with pristine water, land and air. There are trees of all kinds scattered on mountains and in valleys. The flowers are gorgeous, the meadows are lush and the water sparkles. We communicate telepathically with all of nature here. It is very common for us to talk with the water and feel its vibration and love for its life. Leia particularly delights in these interactions and is studying this intensely, so she can teach visitors to the Pleiades how we communicate with our environment.

We live extremely comfortably here and all of our needs are met; we do not struggle to survive. We are not employed but have jobs we like and enjoy participating in. The word "job" is loosely translated because even though the jobs here are different from yours, the word "job" in the third dimension sometimes has an energy of burdensome work for little money. We, of course, do not have, need, or want money.

We, our environment and the stars are in tranquility. The trees know they will live a life of pleasure. No one will cut them down. The waters sparkle; no one will pollute them. There are few animals here, but those that are know they will not be killed for consumption.

Please know that we understand the cutting of trees and the consumption of animals. We understand the chain of life in the third dimension. We view it all with love. We honor your life ways and want to stay in ours!

The Pleiades is always a perfect temperature. There are no storms, earthquakes, or volcanoes. We have beings here who continually work through thoughts and energy to maintain balance in our star system.

All our relationships here are loving. Some of the Pleiadians on Earth miss that. Relationships on Earth can come with expectations and rules that do not always feel so good.

Our relationships are important to us. We complement and support each other. Although we are always connected telepathically, we enjoy being with each other in the physical. We like to pray together. We like to meditate together. We like to celebrate together. Pleiadians are very social and we like to be in groups. We don't get lost in a group; the group energy accentuates who we are individually and, in turn, powers the group.

I have a home in the Pleiades and I do lots of traveling, visiting and socializing. I visit P'taah's home, my sister's and brother's homes, and my friends' and colleagues' homes here, in the galaxy and the universe. Part of my work is to know and become familiar with life outside this galaxy and universe. I enjoy seeing new places and meeting other beings.

The population in the Pleiades is small, less than a million. We are spread out over the stars, some beings live in small villages and many live in the country. Our home is not crowded. We look at the Earth and we see many areas that have more people than our entire star system has.

It's normal for us to talk with our environment and I know some of the Starseeds are missing those relationships and interactions. We value all of nature. Our homes are eco-friendly. They are rounded and open inside. They contain areas for meditation and lounging. We do not physically tax our bodies the way you do, plus we are in a higher, supportive vibration, so we do not need sleep. We do lay down for meditation and dream sleep. We can close our eyes, work with our dream master and experience any loving creation possible. It is quite nice!

Because we do not consume food, there are no kitchens in our home. We have a small area that holds water and other light substances for consumption. It is for enjoyment only; we do not need the support of the intake. We drink a Pleiadian champagne occasionally, which has a base of liquid light. We do have a family room that we gather in for social, humorous times and for sharing galactic adventures.

Our temples look like some of the holy temples on the Earth. These sacred places do not have the religious connotations that Earth temples have. We don't have religion here. The work we do in the temples includes the use of crystals. Some of the crystals have been formed into beautiful windows that compose the walls of the structure.

The crystals enhance our spiritual work and are used in many different areas. I am a teacher in alchemy and use the crystals for acceleration. I can work magic!

You would be very happy to be in the Pleiades. There is peacefulness that you have never experienced on the Earth. It is a knowing that all your needs are met, that you are always cared for and always loved. There is no fear; there is no lack.

BoStro, Oshala and I played games together when we were children. We would run around the Pleiades and play tag. It was on a much grander scale. In the Pleiades, we think and we are, so you can imagine what tag was like!

I am loyal and dedicated to my sister and will stay with her through all time. I have never had an unkind, unloving thought about my sister; it is not possible for me to think of one. I hold her in the highest regard and am forever with her. I love her.

I am lingering now because I like being so close to my dear sister. She would probably never have channeled me if it weren't for this book. I, too, was whispering in her ear, "Write a book."

Because I knew when she saw me, she would channel me. My love is clever.

Always in love,

I am Aaron

Oshala – With Unconditional Love

Greetings, this is Oshala.

My life in the Pleiades is complete love and enjoyment; it is exquisite. As you are interacting with me, you are feeling all the energies of love that are experienced in the higher dimensions. You are interacting with unconditional love, acceptance, support and happiness.

You are sensing all the love that I have around me and all the love I have for you in all times that is unconditional and constant. As you have discovered, sometimes love on the Earth is conditional.

I can hear you thinking, "Well, what about me? Why am I not always loved? Why am I not always supported?"

Sometimes you think, "Well, the love is coming, but what's it going to cost me? How much do I have to give? How hard is this love going to be?"

You desire love and acceptance, but often there's a price to pay for that. I, Oshala, don't have to pay a price, but I know some of you have, and that can be very difficult on your heart. Kate has paid a price from time to time and after she paid it, the love was not love at all. It was fear.

Sometimes love in duality doesn't feel good. Humans can experience love and still be in fear. I hear your thoughts about all the different energies of love and how it can be entwined and convoluted at times.

Your experiences have made you suspicious of love. Sometimes you put conditions on the love you offer to others and sometimes they put conditions on you. The polarizations and duality on Earth make love seem complicated. There's a lot going on with love, when really, love is so simple.

Sometimes people conditionally love themselves. They hold back on self love and this too is hard on their hearts. Being hard on yourself is just that: you are hard on yourself. And this helps in no way. Please do not do this, please do not be hard on yourself. This hardness was taught by those who do not want you to know who you really are. You know who you really are, and I will tell you again, you are love, loved and loving.

The perceived separation and all that it entails has been difficult. You came from a place of acceptance with a feeling of belonging. You were part of the Oneness. You still are part of the Oneness, but life in duality has shaken your beliefs. Now you must work to regain that sense of belonging and love while on Earth. You know you are part of the Oneness, however you do not always feel you are.

I am putting forth the powerful thought, with your permission, that you will be guided to that which will help you grow into an even better place where unconditional love is all there is.

In unconditional love,

I am Oshala and
I am Kate

Leia – Love Your Life

Hi hi hi hi hi. This is Leia. Hello! Hi!

I've been listening to all the conversations especially the ones the readers are having with themselves. I find them fascinating.

My life here is very simple. My life here is great fun. I love who I am and I love who you are, but I don't want to be you. I don't want to be on your planet. I can only take it in small doses because, you know, I just love my life in the Pleiades. And I love myself.

I don't have any of those thoughts or feelings that people on the Earth are thinking. I hear your thoughts and read your minds, and I think, "Oh, I am glad that it's not me!"

As I said earlier, in your terms, I'm about fourteen years old and I love being that age. I see people on the Earth, eight and nine year old girls and they want to be fourteen or fifteen. I see young men, twelve and thirteen, and they want to be twenty. Then I see women at forty who want to be twenty. Then I see men at forty, happy, and they just want to stay forty, but then they turn sixty and they're angry. It's just really baffling. I mean I do understand it, but oh, gosh, where I am, I'm happy being fourteen. I love being in this space and this time.

I loved being eight. And I loved being ten. And I'm sure I'll love being twenty. I've been twenty in many other lifetimes. This isn't my first lifetime in the higher dimensions. I'm an older soul but in this incarnation, I like being fourteen on the Pleiades. And I see sometimes where the Earth people will say, "Well, I was only eight" or they'll make fun of somebody for being ten, saying "Didn't you know that" or,

"My gosh, I learned that in first grade." You know, I don't beat myself up for having been eight or ten years old. I don't beat myself up for not knowing things before I learned them. Learning is joyful—it's exciting!

I'm very enthusiastic. I like every now moment of my life. When I connect with fourteen year old girls from Earth—that's not very frequently, mind you—but when I check in with other fourteen-year-old, young ladies on the planet, they are everywhere but being fourteen. Most of them want to be twenty and they forget what it's like to be fourteen because they are very busy thinking about being sixteen so they can drive. Then they want to be eighteen so they can graduate and get away from home. Then they want to be nineteen so they can go to college and have more fun.

They're hopping all around but I'm happy to be right here, being fourteen.

Today I was playing games. We have spiritual games here, somewhat like a hide-and-seek. And we were running around the meadows with flowers and making fairy essences. I'm very connected to the fairy elements here, the fairy energies, the devas. I work with some of the devas and fairies on the Earth. We do our lessons through games and exercises. One game is a telepathic hide-and-seek, supporting our spiritual gifts, working on telepathic communications with fairies, devas and elementals. We already really know the answers, but it is more fun and it helps us practice our telepathic skills with other beings that aren't quite like us. They're on a different vibration, a different wavelength, so we are practicing with them. And of course everything we do is in fun and it's all in joy. I'm studying and I'm working and I'm learning about these unique beings through a game, through fun.

So we were running around the meadows and flowers, the trees and the streams, working on these skills and, you know, I am very intelligent. I'm very knowledgeable. I have completed a lot of schooling. I have a great ability in science and math and I know a lot about physics. But I am fourteen, I am young. I am enjoying my life. I'm enjoying my time. I'm enjoying being young in the Pleiades.

Some of the adults, some of the older Pleiadians will come by and support us and teach us through games and recreation. And they like to play too! We are enthusiastic about learning here. A lot of the learning on Earth is not like learning in the Pleiades. There is authority on Earth and the young people's power is taken.

Some Earth students are confined in their thinking. Learning is not always cheerful. They are learning to imitate instead of learning to be themselves. In school, the material that they're reading is old and, frankly, a lot of it is inaccurate.

We are always in the truth here. We always have a lot of information and knowledge and it's great fun and we are supported.

Sometimes P'taah will come join our games. He likes to have fun and he's learning something from being with us; he's learning from our learning. It might be similar to grandparents playing checkers with the grandchildren. I said grandparents, because it is not the same as a parent playing with their children. That is something very different and we won't go into that. So I'm fourteen and P'taah, well, he's older, but we're loved whoever we are and wherever we are.

I wish the Earth humans would love themselves more. I would like to teach them, but it's very difficult. I want them to be happier.

But, boy, that's a really big task because there is quite a lot of sadness on the Earth and there's no shortage of people wanting to pull the joy from you and replace it with sadness.

I see the energy in play. I see the auras interact, I see the emotions tangle and so when a high vibration comes in touch with a lower vibration, something's going to happen. It's either they're going to go up to that high vibration or they're going to go down to the lower and usually they go to the lower.

You have to be very strong and keep the high energy up, the high vibration up. It takes practice. It takes awareness. It takes love for yourself. But I can see how you all are loving yourselves more than you were years ago.

I've never had to practice loving myself. But then, I'm not on the Earth—and there's no judgment in that because we came to the Pleiades loving ourselves. We came here knowing everybody loves us, but I know that's not the case on Earth. I have seen babies born unloved and unwanted. So it is kind of difficult, I know. In a way, you have to train yourself. You have to learn.

On a festive note, guess what? I am planning a party with surprises for Kate when I meet her at her Ascension. She has told me many things she would like when she arrives and I have a couple of other surprises too.

I am telling you this because your family has a party ready for you, too. It will be a splendid occasion and if you would like, I can help plan your party. The party is in honor of you. It is a celebration of you!

Well, I'm going to close now. I'm happy where I am, being in love with myself and my life.

I am Leia. Bye!

P.S. I love you too!

♡

Part Three:

P'taah

Channelings of Ascended Master P'taah from the Pleiades

The following are channelings from P'taah that I have done over the last few years. His love and affection at every stage in my life constantly amazes and pleases me. His view is always in love and acceptance. While I have often been unable to accept myself for who I am at a given point in time, P'taah always did, does now, and will continue to do so.

I am in gratitude for his kindness and support of all of who I am.

Love always,

Kate

Greetings

Greetings Star Family, this is P'taah.

Some of you know me. I am P'taah, an Ascended Master and Teacher from the Pleiades. My name is familiar to you and I use this opportunity to connect with you, my family. I am excited to speak with you through the channel and to send you more of my love and support. Meditate on my name and remember me. My name means Teacher of Light. I am your teacher and your guide.

You and I have spent a great deal of time together in the Pleiades. You are advanced beings who have come to Earth at this special time to work with yourselves, humanity and the planet. I have taught you many lessons and I continue to teach you in your dream time. You are Starseeds from the Pleiades, a fifth dimensional star system.

I know many of you wish to leave the planet because the duality and polarizations are too much. You tell me "P'taah, I cannot be here anymore."

I hear you, I hear you all. And I ask you to stay, I ask you to finish your mission and I tell you that you *will* return. You will return to the beautiful Pleiades. Most of you reading this are on your last life on this planet, and I say to you, go for it, go for it all and make it a glorious and spectacular last life.

Please call on me and I will be of great service to you. This is P'taah and I am a member of your real Family.

Remember and Wake Up

You know I see you struggle and I see your strife. And although many of you do not know me by name, you call to the heavens and you reach me.

I look at you and connect with you and send you even more of my love. Would it surprise you that many of you reject my love for you? Yes, Dear Ones, you deny my love for you. You deny me and my love. I see you contract and become hardened and you close off your hearts, making me work even harder to reach you.

But I love my work and I do not tire. For sending love to you is a great joy. Please open your hearts to me and allow me to love you. I will always love you and my love is unconditional. There is nothing you could say or do, or have said or done, that would lessen the love I have for you. I send infinite waves of love to your beautiful and blessed hearts.

Remember and wake up. You are here to fulfill your planetary mission as well as your mission to humanity and Self. You came here with high hopes and great ambitions. I ask you now to remember them and work on fulfilling them. And yes, I know how difficult it can be on the Earth at this time. I hear your calls of distress and I acknowledge them. I return those calls with love and compassion. I feel your heartache and the homesickness that you endure.

And yet, I know that if you left the Earth and came Home, a part of you would still yearn to go back, to be in the sweet energy of service. So I ask you, please work on fulfilling your mission. Follow your path and you will be so proud. You will have the pride that I have when I refer to you as my beloved students.

Close to Home

You are closer to your fifth dimensional Home than you think. You think you are far, but when you think of Home, then you are there. Your fifth dimensional Self is already there and, without realizing or intending to do so, you have connected with that part of yourself, and then the bell ringing of memories of Home come pouring in.

When you think of us, you are activating your memories of Home. When you think of star ships, when you think of the Higher Masters, when you are in Unity Consciousness, those are all aspects of what will soon fully be your Home.

Even with the locks and seals on your consciousness, that feeling of homesickness still creeps in. Rest assured, my Dear Ones, you are on your way back Home.

Feelings and Emotions

Do you remember, Dear Ones, that you came to Earth for the experience of the wide range of emotions that are available for expression here?

And you say, "Well, why would I do that? Why would I want, at times, to experience such lower vibrations?"

And my answer is, "Because you can. Because you can experience feelings and emotions here that do not exist in the higher dimensions."

When you are in the fifth dimension with me, I, as a Spiritual teacher, explain these feelings and emotions to you and you look at me, wondering, "What in the world?"

Then you say, "Well, I will go and experience this for myself, and then I will learn and then I will know." And yes, you have learned.

You have learned and now you are almost finished. I hear your call and request for completion and am happy to say, Dear Ones, you are almost Home.

Conditional Love

I love you unconditionally and always. My love for you is unwavering, even in your most contracted state. No matter what you say, or what you do, my love remains constant and free from conditions.

So I have to ask you, the Ascending Master, do you love unconditionally? Do you have conditions about whom you will love and when you will love? Do you have an "if you do this," or "if you did that" condition?

The old paradigm of using fear energies of control, aggression and competition in being and giving love is not going to fit anymore, Dear Ones. Doesn't that sound strange, using the fear energies with love? And I wonder, how does it feel when you give or receive love that is based in fear?

I Am a Master and You Are a Master

I am one of the Masters and Teachers in the Pleiades. I am also a Master and Teacher on the Earth. I am here with you on Earth and I am here with you in the Pleiades. I had lifetimes on the Earth and I ascended. So a part of me is with you in becoming a Master and part of me is with that part of you that is a Master already.

So, I congratulate you. I congratulate you in all the work you have done and all the work you are doing and all the work you will do. You have made it in future time and in linear time, you are almost there. You are an Ascending Master and you are looked upon with great favor in the galaxies.

I see the final picture and it is beautiful beyond belief. You are in the picture with me and you are happy to be Home, being love.

$\heartsuit$

Open Hearts

You know Dear Ones, you have waited so long for this sacred and special time. You have waited a long time in this lifetime and in other lifetimes. You have studied this time, you have prepared for this occasion. And you told me that in this time you would be open, open to receiving love and giving love.

So why then do I see your hearts closed? Not only are they closed to sending love, they are closed to receiving love. I understand this and yet it is curious to me, as you all know the power of an open heart.

I ask you to forgive your trespasses and to forgive others. Now is not the time to dive more deeply into duality. Love openly and unconditionally. Love as we do and as who you really are.

I send you my love. Will you please receive it? And will you please send some of it to others?

Change

Change is inevitable. Everything changes. The changes in your physical, social, political, financial and technological world will continue to grow at an unprecedented pace. All these changes can be very destabilizing for you.

You call up to me and say, "P'taah, I want something new, I want something better. When is all this going to change for me?" And then you go back to your old ways, your old habits.

I see you resist the change and then I see you wonder when change is coming. I know you hold on to that old memory or that old pattern and you replay it every day, sometimes for years. But even when you resist and do not flow, it is a change. And I wonder, do you like what you have created in this resistance to change?

This is the question I have for you, "When are you going to change? When are you going to shift to create where you want to be? Will you wait until your next life to do that?"

Within Self

You are wondrous, awesome beings who hold the answers to all the questions you ask of Spirit. When I was on Earth, I worked with the mysteries and I worked with the mysteries within myself. I explored the layers and levels of Self with great enthusiasm.

Dear Ones, know who you are. Explore yourselves and look at yourselves through the eyes of unconditional love and acceptance. And you will see what I see, perfect expressions of God in service. And if there is something that you see that you do not like, then call on me and we will look at it with great love. We will work on releasing it and filling the space with the fifth dimensional light that you will return to very soon.

Do You Know Who You Are?

You know that the main lessons on the Earth are taught through relationships. I have talked about this to you many times before. These relationships seem so simple when you are looking at them from your fifth dimensional Self. In fact, you told me then, "Oh yes P'taah, I can handle that. I can handle a relationship based on duality and polarizations. I can do that, no problem."

Now I check in with you and ask, "So how is it going with the relationships? How is the energy between you and your mother? Between you and your father? Between you and your boss?"

You say, "Well, it doesn't feel so good; it's not working like I thought it would."

I ask, "Are you loving yourself? Do you know you are love?"

You stop and wonder, "Well, what does that have to do with my mother and my father and my boss?"

I say to you, "It is all there is."

And then I hear you think and I feel you remember. And then the "aha" moment comes.

So I ask, "Do you know who you are?"

The School of the Mysteries

I, P'taah, would like you to invite me into your lives. I have a great love for you, my students, and I would like to be closer to you.

I have a great deal of information that I would like to share with you. And you might be surprised at what I have to tell you. I can tell you stories from the P'taah School of the Mysteries and you will be amazed and delighted at some of the roles you have played in the galaxies.

I will share these stories with you because I want you to know more of who you are. I would enjoy telling you all the wonderful, magical things you have done. My teaching specialty is relationships and, in particular, the relationship with Self. And I think that experiencing more of who you are in unity would be a great way to experience and love more of yourselves.

Blessed and Happy

You know, Dear Ones, that when you asked, when you applied, when you stood in line to come to Earth you were so happy! You almost could not wait until the adventures began. Your time in preparation was spent saying thank you to many beings. You thanked your soon-to-be teachers, your guides, all your friends everywhere and really, anyone who would listen.

If I were to take you back to see how you were before you came, you would be astounded. You jumped with joy and had continual smiles at what a blessing coming to Earth was.

So now I see that you are not always feeling grateful. And you are not always so happy. And I understand this.

So I tell you of your joy and many blessings so that you remember and feel more of who you really are: joy and love.

As I have told many of you before, this is your last life in this intense duality. Smile at the illusion and give thanks as it has served you well.

We Are All Equal

Do you remember that we are all equal? That you and I are equal. Yes, the teacher and the student are equal. We are on different levels, but we are of equal importance, equal in value. Each of us is as good as the other.

When I connect with your mental body and I hear your internal talk and I read your thoughts about yourself, I see that you like to compare. You compare everything: you compare things to other things and then compare those things to yourself. And then when you finish comparing everything, you start comparing yourself to yourself. Sounds strange, doesn't it?

So I ask you, dear students, to accept things as they are and then as they will be. Work in the now and work in love.

Can You Be Love?

Do you know that *being* is a great service to yourself and the planet? Being the light and the love that you are is a tremendous accomplishment and gift to yourself and the Earth.

I tell you now again, my dear students, that when your life review comes, it will not be based on how much money you made, what type of car you drove, or what your weight was. You will be asked about light and love.

The questions will go like something like this, "Did you love everyone you had contact with? Did you love the planet? Did you love the life you led? Did you send light to all these areas?" And for the grand finale, the last question will be, "Did you love yourself?"

So I ask you, can you *be* light, can you *be* love?

Relationship to Self

I have spoken about relationships many times with you and in many different ways. And I have emphasized the relationship you have with yourself. We talked about this before you came here and we talk about it while you are here. And by the way, you were much more enthusiastic about the subject before you stepped down into duality.

I hear your internal voice and the chatter about yourself. So, in your dream time you meet with me and we review the words and thoughts you are having about yourself. We move in and out of linear time and eavesdrop on conversations between beings. The identity of the beings in the conversation is blocked so you only hear two voices.

And you say to me, "Oh, P'taah, one person is talking so harshly to the other. It does not feel good."

Then I say to you, "Look closer," and you realize it is you talking to yourself.

You are my brave and beloved students and I, P'taah, love you so much. So I ask you to view yourself from my eyes and you will see the wondrous beings of light that you are. And I ask you to view yourself from all there is, love.

A Perfect Expression of God

Do you know how much you are loved? Do you know we look at you and see the miraculous, divine being that you are? We admire you and comfort you and hold you in the highest regard.

And so I ask you, how do you love yourself? Are you loving yourself unconditionally and with complete acceptance? I hear your internal voice talking to you and I wonder if you know how that affects all the parts of yourself. Do you remember that your physical, emotional, mental and spiritual bodies absorb all that you say to yourself and can manifest those words in accordance to what you are saying?-

You are a powerful being with great ability to manifest. Please be kind to yourself and love yourself unconditionally. Tell yourself the things that we tell you, the things that we think of you: that you are perfect, a perfect expression of God.

Loving Your Life

You know I hear you. I hear your words and I hear your heart. Sometimes what I hear is confusing, but then I sit and listen and I process your duality, and then your words and feelings become clearer.

Your words say you want to come Home. You are tired of duality, and bringing unity to the planet was harder than you thought. You say, "I have done my work and I am ready to go. Come and get me. Please."

And then I hear your heart and your heart wants to stay. Your heart wants to love yourself more, love humanity more and love the Earth more. So I say in reply to your calls, "What does your heart feel like doing?"

You struggle a bit and then smile and say to Spirit, "Yes, I will stay."

And I hear you thinking, "Whenever the Ascension comes for me, that is my time. I will do my best not to wait every day for the Ascension. I will live more fully and in a love for everyday life and the experience of it all."

Grounding

So Dear Ones, would you believe that most of you are not in your physical bodies? You are half in or half out and sometimes nowhere near your body. And you say to me, "But P'taah, I just want to leave, to go back to my real Home." But you know, dear students, that you cannot do the work here on Earth that will help you to get back Home if you are not in your body to do the work.

I ask you to ground yourselves and to live in your physical body. This will facilitate your return Home to your fifth dimensional life, your Pleiadian life with your Star Family.

Self Love

You are all beautiful Starseeds doing beautiful heart centered work. When I check in with you, when I connect with your mental body, the first thing I usually hear is that you want to leave. Then I hear you being hard on yourself. Your hearts are often open to everyone but yourself.

Often, even if your heart is open to yourself, it is only ajar and with conditions. I see you love others unconditionally and wholeheartedly, but when it comes to yourself, you hold back with judgment and non-forgivingness.

And now I am asking you, "Can you ease up on yourself? Can you give to yourself the love that you give so easily and freely to others? Can you be all loving?"

Your Planetary Mission

Remember along with your mission to yourself and to humanity, you are also on the Earth to fulfill your mission to the planet. You told me, "Yes, P'taah I can do it, I will work on my mission to the planet. Please let me go to Earth to help her heal and help her ascend. I would like to have a physical experience of being on the third dimensional Earth."

So, this is a reminder to include the Earth in all parts of your life. She wants to be involved in your life on her. She participates actively with you, even when you have not invited her.

Can you imagine how wonderful it will be when you call on your Mother and say, "Please help me and love me even more so I can be of greater service"?

Earth is honored to have human life on her. Show your love by including her in your life in all ways, with love.

♡

In Closing, a Gift

Do you know that you are magnificent, magical beings of light with great creative powers? Your powers are especially strong right now in the gateway of the Ascension. I know many of you and have seen your creations in your Home, in the fifth dimension. And if you could see them and know them as I do, you would be in awe of yourself!

You have worked so hard and so diligently and we are most proud of you, our beloved Starseeds. I am pleased to speak with you today and bring you all a gift. I bring you the gift of remembering that you have infinite possibilities of creation and that I, P'taah, will help you with these miracles of creation. Call on me to be with you and I will help you to increase your powers and you will be most pleased with your work.

May you use this gift with joy and in love,

I am P'taah

♡
_____

Afterword

Thank you for reading *Love from the Pleiades*. You have assisted in bringing more of the Pleiadian light onto the Earth. Their light is beautiful beyond belief. So often I wept in the channelings because it was heart touching, for really all they wanted to say, and all there really is, is love.

Your light is intensely beautiful, too. Your beauty is matched with theirs.

Wishing you to be always in love,

Kate

About the Author

Kate is a spiritual teacher and voice channel for the Ascended Masters. The focus of her readings is on spiritual progression, healing and self empowerment.

She works closely with her Pleiadian Master Teacher and Personal Guide, P'taah, and her Pleiadian Star Family.

Born and raised on a farm in Central Illinois, Kate and her husband currently reside in Arizona on Spruce Mountain, a Lighted Sacred Mountain. This sacred area is connected to the Pleiades and light work is done in their medicine wheel and tipi. A Pleiadian Light Temple is soon to be built. They both work in the Pleiadian Starseeds Center in Prescott.

You may find out more about Kate and her work at KateSparks.com.

You may also email her at Kate@KateSparks.com.

Notes

Printed in Great Britain
by Amazon

17157186R00071